FINISHING LINE PRESS

www.finishinglinepress.com

February's Rose

poems by
Bing Hua

translated by
Yingcai Xu

Finishing Line Press
Georgetown, Kentucky

February's Rose

Publisher: Leah Huete de Maines
Editor: Christen Kincaid
Cover Art: Bing Hua
Author Photo: Bing Hua
Translator Photo: Yingcai Xu
Cover Design: Elizabeth Maines McCleavy

Order online: www.finishinglinepress.com
also available on amazon.com

Author inquiries and mail orders:
Finishing Line Press
P. O. Box 1626
Georgetown, Kentucky 40324
U. S. A.

Table of Contents

I. The Sunflower

1. The Sunflower 1
2. The Karma from a Song 3
3. Sonata on Karma 4
4. To the Plane Tree 5
5. The Sound of Silence 6
6. A Tender Affection for the South 8
7. Quantum Entanglement 10
8. If I Were Wind 11
9. Neither out of Flighty or Levity 12

II. February's Rose

10. The Sensational Touch of January 15
11. My Longing for You Is like Snow 16
12. February's Rose 17
13. The Peach Orchard in March 18
14. March Peach Blossoms that Beautify Each Other 19
15. Spring 21
16. Spring Breeze 22
17. Mayflowers 23
18. The Amorous Knot of June 24
19. The Light of Time 25

III. That Summer

20. I Am 29
21. Please Take a Good Care of the Bird 30
22. Skidding Pebbles upon the Water 31
23. Walk and Walk 32
24. To Fly 33
25. Lily in the Drizzle 34
26. Pray 35
27. Drifting 36
28. Drinking Coffee 37
29. That Summer 38
30. This Girl 39

31. Plucking the Rose 40
32. Wind 41
33. Confession 42
34. The Sorrow of Blue 43
35. When I Got to the Seashore 44
36. When I Turn Seventeen 45
37. The Cost of a Word 46
38. The Reflective Sound Wall 47
39. An Eagle 48

IV. The Lotus' Obsession

40. The Lotus' Obsession 51
41. Alley 52
42. Flirtatious 53
43. A Life-long Cherished One 54
44. That Door 55
45. If 56
46. Love 57
47. My Prince of the Demons 58
48. Watch You Leave 59
49. Setback 60
50. An Ice Flower 61
51. A Persistent Longing Yet to be Quenched 62
52. The Love Knot 63

V. Never Invest in Love

53. Never Invest in Love 67
54. Haunting Thoughts 68
55. Waiting 69
56. The Rebirth of a Tree 70
57. The Autumn Bride 71
58. An Amorous Spring Night 72
59. Exorbitant Expectation 73
60. There Is Such Love 74
61. Twin Flowers on One Stalk 75
62. Understanding You 76
63. My Love 78
64. Dancing 79
65. Promise 80

66. An Unusual Love 82
67. Let Us Hold Our Hands Forever 83
68. Come on Over 84
69. Why 85
70. Autumn Roses 86
71. Deep Autumn Provoked Deep Longing 87
72. Love Found through the Internet 88
73. To Give Up 89

VI. A Hand Fan

74. A Hand Fan 93
75. Famous Wine 94
76. The Thermos Bottle 95
77. The Drinking Water Bottle 96
78. Startled 97
79. Bridge 98
80. The Fall Wind 99
81. Your Leaves and My Water 100
82. Mood 101
83. A Woman Who Does not Use a Cell Phone 102
84. Leaves and Birds 104
85. The Very Same 105
86. Railway Tracks 106
87. Lotus Root Is the Mercy Buddha 107
88. This Is not Roving 108

VII. The Scarf of the Moonlight

89. The Scarf of the Moonlight 111
90. Gui Fei, the Imperial Beauty, Is Drunk 112
91. Glamorous Photos 113
92. The Firefly 114
93. Fish Begin to Chuckle 115
94. Heavy Snow 116
95. Size 117
96. Teeth 118
97. Dust 119
98. Flowers in Tranquility 120
99. The Blooming and Falling of a Flower 121
100. The Light of Poetry 122

Translator's Notes

When Bing Hua's first Chinese poetry selection *Roses by the Stream* came out, because I was then busy translating a series of prose collections, rarely surfing the internet, I was not aware of it. One day a few years later when I was browsing some webpages, I came across the English translation of one of her poems. Worrying its quality might give negative impression to readers as it was most likely rendered by an American who didn't know Chinese language, I left her a message, asking her not to use that translation. We didn't know each other at that time. So, I had not at all expected that someday the seed I had sown by leaving her a message would have such a butterfly effect as to bloom into the flower of the translation of this *Selected Poems of Bing Hua*.

Last year, the editor in charge of new poems forwarded me some poems she had requested from some well-known poets for the debut issue of *Poetry Hall*, a Chinese and English bilingual journal. I immediately recognized Bing Hua's four poems among them. I was by then already well informed of her poetry writing excellence, but because I felt two of the translations that came with the poems could be improved, I took the liberty and retranslated them into English. Unexpectedly, once I started translating her poems, I could hardly stop, as the butterfly effect took its full wing. I am a translator and a poet as well. Once I see good poems, how can I stop translating them? Therefore, I asked her to send me another eight love poems. I translated them and published them in the Special Column of our *Poetry Hall*.

By now, we already knew each other well. I loved her poems and she adored my translation. Although I was very busy and wanted to translate some classical Chinese works, once she asked me to translate this Selected Poems of Bing Hua, I put aside everything I was doing and immediately accepted her request.

A summer lotus bud, yet to bloom
Has an obsession wrapped in its heart
Who can peel off those wrapping petals
Who can call out the wrapped heart

Most of Bing Hua's poems, if not all, are inspired by nature. They are vivid in image, authentic in feeling, unique in artistic concept, and clear in internal rhythm, such as the above-mentioned free verse The Lotus' Obsession.

Once you read it, the image of an obsessed lotus bud and its artistic concept would linger in your mind for a long time. Bing Hua's poetic language is characterized with a unique freshness. Wherever you come across it, you can easily identify it as Bing Hua's language.

In translating this selection, I strive to render her poems as poems, to use words as colors to paint the images she has projected, and to use translation as a medium to convey the feelings she wants to convey, focusing on bringing out her poetic individuality or style, so familiar readers can recognize her poems as hers through the translation. On top of Yan Fu's three words translation guidelines I follow— faithfulness, expressiveness, and elegance, I also strive to fulfil my own translation principle: accuracy, individuality, and coherence. But as this translation is done with quite a limited amount of time, there must be some mistakes. I beg your forgiveness, if so.

Yingcai Xu

I. The Sunflower

1. The Sunflower

Is a newborn baby's
Sweet smile in its dream
Or the flower of youth
In bud ready to bloom
—No
It's an ancient Greek nymph
Clytie
In love with the Sun

She loves him
So her heart turns toward him
From sunrise to sunset.

She loves him
So she looks up to him
Till her hair turns grey

Near or far
It's measured by light
Faithful and true
It's witnessed by Heaven and the Earth.

Van Gogh's Sunflower
Has a set value
But Clytie's
Is priceless

O
My Apollo
I love you
But conceited as I am
I can't utter
The word love

All my love
Has gone hidden
In Van Gogh's paintings

My love
Is that of Clytie's
And Clytie's
Is
The sunflower

2. The Karma from a Song

Through a song of our likes
My soul encounters yours

Though I've never seen you
I'm well acquainted with your present and past lives
Though I've never heard your voice
I'm happily disposed to your advice

You
Stand atop a mountain summit
Amid white clouds
Gazing far into the distance
Chanting alone

I
Atop another mountain summit
Of the same height
Feel your heartbeat
Humming a duet with you

I raise my right hand
And from over my head push the cloud
To you
So the two clouds collide
Your eyes
Shine with delight

The sky and water
Are in one blend of color
You and I
Are mesmerized by one same song
My mountain and your mountain
Resound with the same melody

3. Sonata on Karma

Encountering someone at the wrong time
Forfeits the opportunity to acquaint with him
Meeting someone at the right time
Embroiders a new epic

If your sorrow
Is my sorrow
If your dismay
Is my dismay
How can I not love
What you have gone through

If your pursuit
Is my pursuit
If your longing
Is my longing
How can I not love you
From your head to toe

You are a mirror
In which I can see myself clear
You've woken me up
From my slumber
You've turned the moon
Into the sun
How can I not
Be thankful to Heaven

Look
Our sail
Is cruising into the harbor of love
Tear after tear
They roll into the sea
Gull after gull
They soar into the sky
You and I—
Our encounter
Will bloom into the rainbow at the edge of sky

4. To the Plane Tree

If I love you
I'll have my feathers
Grow green
To harmonize with your color
So I'm part of your emerald

If I love you
I'll turn myself into the queen of all the birds
When they fly to me
I'll lead them to you

And
I'll declare to them
To the blue sky, to the white clouds, and to the green tree
You are not only the king of the plane
You are also my king

My King of Plane
Only
The phoenix, the Queen of all birds,
Can be your bride
Can be your queen

5. The Sound of Silence

On the busy modern street
Who runs to the spring of heart

Bathing in the morning rays of materials
And keeping off from the moonlight of sexual desire
Loneliness
Is the biting wind of winter

Long black hair
That drifts in the wind
Lacerates the air

When the sound of silence
Wafts over from the distance
Nobody can hear it
That is the gurgling of a rill
And the throbbing of a mountain

It turns out
To be a heart duet
Not an illusion
Nor a dream
But a heavenly melody from a swan-made heart

The celestial clouds
Sentimentally moved by the terrestrial passion
Begin to shed tears like rain

The terrestrial passion
In love of the blue sky
Begins to rise in the form of vapor

The tangle of the tree and vine
Is indeed a virtual love
In the actual world

As long as the heart of silence

In the distance
Pulsates for you
There is no need to be with each other
Love
Is then not beyond love
And the sorrow of love
Will be beyond sorrow

6. A Tender Affection for the South

The south
Used to be the northerner Bing Hua's
Unreachable dreamland

In her dream, the south appears to be
White walls under dark roof tiles
Temples with ancient pagodas
Deep courtyards
With highly raised lanterns

Stone streets and narrow alleys
"A small bridge, a creeping creek, and a few houses
A homesick person roaming on a remote land"

Under an oilpaper umbrella
The beauty who cherishes these southern features
Comes along, sweetening ten miles of lotus flowers

Riding the moon and treading the clouds
The northerner Bing Hua
Comes drifting to the south

In the love legends handed down from ancient times
The southern land abundant with fish and rice
Is now a land as picturesque as a wash painting of love
And the world of mortals with cooking smoke rising
Now a drizzle-mystified wonderland

In the misty drizzle
Bai Niangzi and Xu Xian
Liang Shanbo and Zhu Yingtai
Lu Xiaoman and Xu Zhimo
Manifest themselves now and then

The northerner Bing Hua
In the southern misty drizzle
Walks into the painting of love

The southern misty drizzle
Fulfils her dream
Bing Hua's dream
Is no longer just a dream
But has blended itself
Into the cloud and fog

If
She had not fallen in love with the south
How could she
Blend herself into the southern misty drizzle
If
She had not felt the southern pulsating beats
How could she turn herself into the southern misty drizzle

7. Quantum Entanglement

In the sky
Two stars
Attract each other through gravity

On the ground
Two trees
Though separated by mountains and rivers
Feel the breath from each other

On the earth
The North and South Poles
Though opposite to each other
Rotate on the same heart beat

The Atlantic
And Pacific
Though separated by land
Come from the same source

Isn't this
Karma
Isn't this
Quantum Entanglement

In October, on this terrestrial land
A lady
Stands in the colorful autumn
Gazes
The reflections in the tranquil lake
And appeases

The surging waves in her heart

8. If I Were Wind

If I were wind
I would fly to spring
To green dormant grass
To open flowers
So, I could fall asleep in the flower scent

If I were wind
I would fly to the sea
To splash the waves
To wake up the morning sun
So, I could hear water sing in the first rays

If I were wind
I would fly and fly
Till I alight on his shoulders
If I were wind,
I would blow and blow,
To blow my love into his heart

This is because
He is my spring
My great sea
My distant future
My justification
To wish myself
                To be wind

9. Neither out of Flighty or Levity

Rivers overflow banks
Willow strings stroke water
This is neither out of flighty or levity

Ocean waves embrace beaches
Wave splashes caress reefs
This is neither out of flighty or levity

II. February's Rose

10. The Sensational Touch of January

The afternoon windows
Have ushered the sun's radiance into the hut
The dormant trees
Indulge in the remembrance of their year's long adventures

January's breeze
Flutters what time has touched
That unseasonable snow
Has muted the birds' twittering
Those dried tears and laughs
Have added their weight to the life

I clip a piece out of the sky
And knead some clouds onto it
To put it in my computer

Therefore
I see you on the other distant end
Still watching me

How to lock up my soul
So, it doesn't drift to you
How can I break away from my longing
So, it doesn't fly to you

The sensational touch of January
On the susceptible spot of my soul
Is heading on an unreturnable path
Although roots hurt when detached from the four seasons
Because love is sinless, I'll follow you through any infliction

11. My Longing for You Is like Snow

—Written on Valentine's Day

How I wish I could be snowflakes
To alight on your shoulders
With a few banks of green willows to brush away your chilliness

How I wish I could sing you a love song
And include you in the vocal descriptions
But it turns out I am the only listener indulged

To listen to the song, to listen to the rustling winter wind
With a tightly concealed feeling
I Look at your face, that is familiar and strange
My heart is stung by a rose brought over from afar

Again and again, we meet in dreams
Dream after dream, will they only be dreams?
Inside and outside the dreams, a seed has melted February's ice
And has once burst open silently behind you

Inside and outside the dreams, I tailor my longing into drizzle
To let it fall into poems in a chilly windy night
I'm not clear when my poetic inspiration will come and when go
I'm only aware that my longing for you is like snow, yet the snow never falls

12. February's Rose

My heart
Is filled with February's longing
I want to pull it out
And weave it into a rose garland
To hitch to your heart

My love
Is stung by a February's rose
I want to bear the pain
While brew red wine with it to color my lips
And kiss you to strengthen your love

February's rose
Will trade countless waiting nights
For just a moment to have a heart-to-heart talk with you
So the empathy in our hearts will bloom into a love chemical

February's rose
Will trade countless daydreams
For you to come into my dreams
I'll have no regret, no complaint, and no sorrow

February's rose is like flame
That will warm up the chilly moon on winter nights
And set its greyness ablaze with a riot of colors
That will spread over the sea from shore to shore

13. The Peach Orchard in March

Cool drizzle
Has wet the earth somewhere
The breeze that wafts over like curtain strings
Has kept off the spring radiance of March

In just a few days, peach trees
Will be dressed up in ostentatious red
A twig of delicate fragrance
Has not yet found a tree to graft on

Wind and rain whisper to each other
But no word is mentioned about the peach orchard
When the wind comes again next month
It will ruffle the petals on the ground

Like tears, raindrops perch on the deep end of the wind
But who will pick up the petals
Each of which has recorded
The debt the wind owes

14. March Peach Blossoms that Beautify Each Other

In March
The sky
Is as blue as the sea
Clouds
As white as a wedding gown

You wave your hand
Row after row of trees
Turn green
You smile
Cherry and peach blossoms
Rush to flush

The wind of March
Is light and soft
Your bright eyes
Abash the cherry blossoms
Your smiles
Tipsify the tidal waves and the lake's scene
Your bosom
Like the sun
Has melted the winter ice

An eagle
Stretches out his wings in the sky
Two colorful birds
Dance amid flowers

You are
The morning glow of March
Lingering on the window curtains
You are
One March late afternoon's
Scent of famous tea
You are
One March evening's
Twitters from the home-returning swallows

You are
The poetic cadence ringing in my dream
You and I
Are March peach blossoms that beautify each other

15. Spring

I wonder what type of fan spring uses
That has fanned the grass green and flowers red
I wonder what type of comb spring uses
That has spruced up the gardens and streets

I only see
A fresh and bright rose in the garden
Blooming in the most eye-catching place
A wedding float in the street
Coming from where birds come

O, spring, you are so sweet and charming
I want to be the bride of spring too

16. Spring Breeze

Snowflakes
Have melted
Love
Remains young

Annual ring grows
In wind
Drifts the old tree barks
Blight trees
Heal
In the shower of spring breeze

What spring breeze has blown down
Is rain
What the old trees have shed down
Are tears

If
Spring breeze
Has brought with it the sense of first love
How can the old trees
Not shed tears

In the spring breeze
Wafts over
The scent of dinner
O
Hope it's not a dream

Wrap
The love in the spring breeze
The spring breeze
Is Filled up with my sense of love
The spring breeze with love is the most beautiful
Spring breeze
The beautiful spring breeze
Lightly
Wafts to where cooking smoke rises

17. Mayflowers

Strange, familiar
Remote, intimate
It's an indescribable distance in between each pair

Let me wander in the strangeness
So, I can read you in my dreams
From spring to winter

Let me fly to the remote distance
So, I can watch you from the other river bank
From dusk to the dawn in sunglow

In fact, what I want is
The familiarity I've gained in my dreams
The intimacy I've obtained in my poems
If I'm banned from indulging in such a little fantasy
I'll not understand the distance between life and death

Because I watch you admiringly from a cliff
I have no space to backup
Because the sea dominates the little stream
This is either a man's will or Heaven's

Watch the mayflowers
To be showered in the rain of chagrin
Are they still blessed with the initial beauty in the rain?
A pair of colorful butterflies dance in the storm
The mayflowers' tears strike percussion

18. The Amorous Knot of June

Closer and closer, the blue sky
Walks on white clouds into my heart

In June's garden
Every night, new plants sprout
Every morning, new flowers bloom

June's ocean
Is a dream to embrace the blue sky
Is a wing to heave splashes

A white sail glides to the distance
Lightly and evenly stretching out
The colors of the blue sky and the ocean

On the wind-touched riverbank
Two coconut palms stand hand in hand
But cannot tie the amorous knot

19. The Light of Time

Time
Is a winding path
Where desired scenes
Are always missed
So many windings
So many misses
That they shy me from moving on

The setting sun dips in the west
A flint sparks at a strike
The glowing clouds
Amaze me
And the desired scene
Suddenly emerges

But
The moonlight
Together with its time infliction
Has drenched into the roots of my hair

The unshedable tears
Have wash-shaped the winding path
Into a harbor

From there
A spring-filled boat sails out
That forms a long-dreamed scene
And a new legend

Under the moonlight
The white hair-roots
Are now more flamboyant than red roses
They are
The roses of time
That emit the radiant sunlight of life

III. That Summer

20. I Am

I'm a foolish girl
Who, in escaping a maze
Has stumbled into the bosom of godly romance

I'm a crystal girl
Who, transparent inside out
Is wandering in the Garden of Eden

I'm a susceptible girl
Who, through mutable weather
Has learned how searing the after-storm peace can be

I'm a tenderhearted girl
Who fears to hear the murmur of the breeze
And the rustle of the falling petals on the shady path

I'm a girl with a pure soul
Who doesn't want her whiteness smeared
But saves it for her gifted artist

I'm an exhausted girl
Who is like a boat berthing at a bay
Dazzled by thousands of racing sails

I'm an emotionally weak girl
Who can hardly stand an autumn chill
And the golden smiles of harvest

I'm a wingless girl
Who cannot soar into the ideal azure sky
But tailgate the clouds on a long wind

I'm a girl who finds it hard to say "No"
The wind sways the grass
Where she hides her "No"
That's why you've never found the word

21. Please Take a Good Care of the Bird

Your melody rings out a message of love
The message turns into honey in my heart
The honey drips to form a poem
The poem sends out a bird
And the bird flies into your heart to nest
Please take a good care of the bird

22. Skidding Pebbles upon the Water

One after another
I skid the pebbles across the water
To measure its distance
The merry surface
Blooms into ripples
That expand and expand and expand
To relay rings upon rings of affections

I keep skidding and skidding and skidding
While the sun, the moon, and the stars keep revolving

23. Walk and Walk

Walk and walk
Until your hair turns silvery
When you turn around
You have someone right behind you

Walk and walk
Until you are exhausted like a burnt down candle
When you need to lean
You have someone right by your side

Walk and walk
On this passion-paved road
I'll follow you forever
No matter where we reach
You are always my guide

No need to ask
The answer is long written
Right in our hearts

24. To Fly

The memories of joy
Are no longer joy
Yet the memories of loneliness
Make you feel even more lonely

A passionate love
Is like a kite with a snapped string
And will never fly

Nothing is wrong with the wind
What's wrong
Is the missing of you the driving string

Please reopen my dust-covered dream
And reconnect your string to it
So my dream has a pair of wings

Look, what an azure sky
My dream
Longs to fly

25. Lily in the Drizzle

How to
In her blooming prime
Catch your eyes
For this, she has lit up a thousand incense sticks
And rehearsed ten thousand poses

The lily stands there
With a pious red heart
For you
The fine drizzles
Are the falling of her crystallized longing

Life span is as thin as a piece of paper
So is one's blooming adolescence
Don't wait till the hair turns grey
And then regret the chance you've missed

Oh, the lily in the drizzle
Is longing for her love

26. Pray

I know
In this mundane world
Suffering abounds while joys are scarce
I know
In this mundane world
Parties will end, flowers wither, and trees age

But still I will pray
Pray for a piece of innocent and happy memory
Pray for a permanent and profound love
And pray to have a happy ending for the performance of life

27. Drifting

A small boat
Drifts in the sea
By a mere chance
You turn into its helmsman

You steer the boat into the paradise of dream
On its green island
I've tried all my tenderness to keep you
But still you step out of the boat into the declining sunlight

Your trip may be one-way
Without its helmsman
This boat begins to drift
And drift

28. Drinking Coffee

You are coffee
And I am the ingredients
We dissolve
In the same cup
Our love
Dilutes bitterness with sweetness

Drinking this cup of coffee
You will exude fragrance
I will exude fragrance
The fragrance manifests me
The fragrance manifests you

29. That Summer

That summer, I'm spruced up—
Pink dress
Bangs hanging down to the eyebrows
Short hair cut to the ears
Long eyelashes that
Curve over the two watery eyes

No application of lipsticks
Nor rouge
A pair of pink silk socks
In a pair of T-shaped sandals

I Sneak out of my home
Unnoticed, to look for him
Quietly sitting and waiting
In the alley where he might appear

He appears
I blush
And don't know what to do with my hands
And blurt out some senseless words

He is gone
Sparkling tears roll down my cheeks
Behind him

30. This Girl

This girl
Weaves a garland with roses

You, like fleeting sunlight
Bathe it with a shower of kisses
And then move away
Leaving it a dream and illusions

This girl
In courting the fleeting sunlight
Turns away from the splendor of rainbows

This girl
Longing unfulfilled
Love unexpressed
To see the sunlight again
Resumes her kneel before the Buddha

And her garland weaving for her dream

31. Plucking the Rose

I just want one rose
Although you've given me
A whole garden.
Of so many flowers
Which is the most beloved?
Or should I pick?
It is indeed a hard choice to make
So my tears roll down

They fall to the side of my skirt
Onto the shy stamen
Of a thorny rose
Are they dewdrops
Or tears?

32. Wind

Wind blows
My skirt flares
Oh, wind
Don't say the word "LOVE" to me
It's too light yet too heavy
For my delicate hands
To carry

33. Confession

I am
A person of feeling
My pure passion has kindled
My adolescence
But for a wrong person

I am
A person of one mind
My heart has never been dust-smeared
But is sealed with him
In it

34. The Sorrow of Blue

Quietly I walk off the campus
To the beach
To watch the boundless sea
The endless annoyance
Reigning over my racing heart
In which
Bygone events flutter …

Enlightened by Buddha
I possessed a Buddha-type of kind heart
Only to accidentally trip and fall
To the Cupid's side

So, the dream of love
Had to flee in the blink of an eye
For he who stepped off the bedroom
Was only a friend rather than a lover

No sorrow can be more profound than a moribund heart
The reef under the water
Has smashed all my passion …

The surging sea-waters
The running sorrowful tears
The ocean is blue
And the sorrow too is blue

35. When I Got to the Seashore

No, no, I'd better stop right here
The sea is so boundlessly indistinct
Let me just hide my ardent hope

No, no, I'd better stop right here
I will just leave a picture
To let it accompany the sea

No, no, I'd better stop right here
I can't swim
What's awaiting is more or less death

No, no, I'm not afraid of death
What I'm afraid of is
Without me, the sea will be tempestuous
Rather than peaceful

36. When I Turn Seventeen

Like emeralds, the past feelings
Are laid out in the deepest recess of my soul
Glittering with deep green lights on the other bank of time

Where a girl in a pink skirt
With a heart yet to be cultivated
Often wandered on the grassland
Although longed and dreamed
She could never enter
That ivy-twined door

While sunlight and starlight alternate
Tears roll down onto the music strings
Sparkling, salty, and reticent

The life-long blooming image of adolescence
Has painfully overshadowed the meadow of life
The sweetness of seventeen will linger for the whole life

37. The Cost of a Word

For the word I want
I've spent a year waiting
Once I have the word
It costs my whole life

38. The Reflective Sound Wall

The song I sing to it from my heart
Cannot get through
It simply reflects back what I've said
But fails to reflect
What I've lost in my heart

39. An Eagle

An eagle
Flies in the blue sky
Is she following her lover
Or just returning home

On her left are mountains
Behind her, ranges
In front, a plain
And on her right, a sea
The sea is misty
The seagull's family is busy
So the eagle, where are you heading to

On the earth shimmers the autumn color
In green, red, yellow clusters
So the eagle, where are you perching on

Here comes the wind
That blows her a little off the balance
With a few whistles
And a few circles
She soars far and high

The eagle flies and flies

IV. The Lotus' Obsession

40. The Lotus' Obsession

A summer lotus bud, yet to bloom
Has an obsession wrapped in its heart
Who can peel off those wrapping petals
Who can call out the wrapped heart

People not karma-bound to her
Have either rushed by too quickly
Or arrived too late

For while waiting
Her amorous heart has turned into bitter seeds
An irreversible plight

The lotus' obsession
Remains, though her root is pocketed with holes

41. Alley

In May or June
Fine drizzle and soft breeze
Come into the slumbering alley
Dreamland-like stories are written all over the wall

A girl emerges at the window
To bathe herself in the afternoon sunrays
A pair of eyes appear at the end of the alley
Bright and ardent as July

Gazing from May or June
To the distant October or November
On that wall in that small alley
Is written another beautiful story

42. Flirtatious

Treading on this small globe
Amid the human crowds is an unsettled familiar figure

Who has traded a thousand years of seclusion
For the wickers of a hundred years' growth
To weave a colorful bridge of love

Once I come to know the longing I had in my past life
I begin to dislike my present appearance
So, I linger on and on in the sea of flowers
Praying to turn as fair as Khloris' or Cynthia's

Turning the power preserved for a whole winter
Into wind, I blow up the hem of your garment
Saving the delicate scent for a whole summer
I seduce you to my side

Buds bloom into the flowers of floating rhymes
That fly to your mailbox
Yet before they arrive
I begin to be nervous
So, what you will read is my tender shyness

You've made me so flirtatious

43. A Life-long Cherished One

With the cold astuteness of winter
You've brought me a lake of summer scenes
A sky full of stars are asleep
But I'm the only one awake
Watching and reading you till dawn breaks

You come from the horizon
That is as far as an overnight
You come from amid the splendor of clouds
With a halo exhibiting five colors

You come from the internet
Spreading the feelings of an azure sky
You are a voluminous classic
I find it hard to detach from you

I
In a woman's soft voice
Declare to the whole world
You are my life's most beautiful encounter
And I desire to be your life-long cherished one

44. That Door

The door I longed for
How I wished it could open for me

From nighttime to daytime
After half-a-life-long longing
I finally saw it open

I dared not enter it
But only quietly hoped
With tears in my eyes

That door is closed
Together with the pain
That has hurt me for half a life long

That door
Forms the gravity of my whole life
And the pursuit of three lives

The door I have longed for
Will it open for me again
Let me trade the rest of my life
For a chance to walk through

45. If

If my love
Turns into your burden
If my wholehearted calling
Cannot change your mind
Please make sure you let me know
I'll chose to quietly leave you

I'll adapt myself to a new life
A life without you in it
And I'll also try to figure out the reason
Why my sincere efforts
Gain almost no return
Although I'll still keep you in my heart
And keep praying
For your safety

When you linger in your twilight years
Recalling your past love life
If I have left you even a little remembrance
If so
My solitude-inflicted life
Will not be the one with slightest complaint

46. Love

Is there any such love
After leaving you
I become a pair of caring eyes behind you
Before the cold wind comes
I put a cloak on you

Is there any such love
After leaving you
I become a hand for you
Before the rain comes
I hold up and umbrella for you

Is there any such love
After leaving you
I turn the past pledges
Into fulfilment through others
Without your awareness

Is there any such love
After leaving you
I swallow all the blames
For you
For a better tomorrow

47. My Prince of the Demons

You are my prince of the demons
Like a dagger, your eye-contact
Cores me

You recklessly
Stroll in my soul
Continuously flashing your radiance
And singing chants to me

You are my prince of the demons
Like an arrow, your eye gaze
Shoots through my demureness and disguise

At your unrestrained passion
I have nowhere to hide
Amid your roses
Will I be stung again

You are my prince of the demons
Your blood, my poison
Your frost, my tears
You are my prince of the demons

My prince of the demons
Let you and I
Flame in the blaze of the roses

48. Watch You Leave

Watching your back fade away into the distance
My heart trembles
How I wish you would turn around
And leave me a wisp of tenderness
But you are you
I see you off with tear-swamped eyes
Oh, so cold! Is this
A scorching summer
Or an ice-cold winter

49. Setback

Trees turn green
Flowers turn red
The young girl's love is in full bloom

But followed by "autumn wind"

Trees are no longer green
Flowers are no longer red
Then gone is the spring
And wilted the girl's love

50. An Ice Flower

I'm an ice flower
Blooming in the cold
How I wish you were that sun
To evaporate the chilly frost in your palm

But you turn into wind
To whip my sparkle
Into shards—Oh, so cold I can hardly talk
But a broken ice flower is still an ice flower
While you've lost your shines forever

I can still say
My love is not melted
But you will no longer be him
A broken ice flower is still an ice flower

51. A Persistent Longing Yet to be Quenched

The dust of longing
Thickens and thickens
The tears of sorrow
Accumulate day by day

Many years later
The dust
Has attained the thickness of the earth's crust
The tears
Have reached the depth of a river

The heavy earth
The roaring river
Converge
To return to my heart

The dust and the tears
The earth and the river
Combine
To give birth to poem after poem

Every poem
Is yet an unquenched longing

The one who has longed
And the one who has been longed for
As a result of different personalities
Have been torn up by time

The one who has longed
And the one who has been longed for
Have finally been torn apart by the god of fate

The one who has longed
And the one who has been longed for
Have turned out to be strangers as they were

52. The Love Knot

Is it my obsessed feeling that has moved you
Or is it you who still think of me
Otherwise why do you always come in my dreams
Despite wind or rain

Time and again you've listened to my sleep talk
Time and again you've read my secrete
But when I move a little bit closer to you
You rush away
Where can I find you

I am no longer me
You are no longer you
Such a dream
Is meaningless
Who can tell me
What a dream really is
And what love really is

When I wake up from my dream
I don't know where I am
Then again I cheat myself
By saying that I've never loved you

The repeated dream
You are my only
Repeated dream
That has haunted me for ten years
And will remain even after a hundred years

My dream lover
You are my only
Dream and love
That form an unraveling knot

V. Never Invest in Love

53. Never Invest in Love

Apart from love
All is marketable
And any loss re-gainable

Apart from love
All is cultivable
And any land harvestable

In the dictionary of love
There is no entry for the word of affection

Love is simply like photographing
Moment freezes eternity
No law of quantity to quality is involved
Neither the balance between investment and productivity

Love is a losing stock
Any one-sided decision to buy in
Will finally be caught up
Whatever investment you make, better not love

54. Haunting Thoughts

I scoop the water-like tender feeling
In my hands
But am afraid it might slip through my fingers

I cradle the sun-like warming passion
In my arms
But am afraid the sun might move away

I wrap the wind-like passionate affection
Around my body
But am afraid the wind may blow it away

I plant flower-like burning love
In the vase
But am afraid the flower may wither

I hang the moon-like insatiate longing
Over the window
But am afraid the moon might sail into the clouds

I lower my head
Flowing over the piano keys are these sorrows

55. Waiting

When I miss you
I burn an incense
And pray for your good health and wellbeing

When I miss you
I stroke your pictures
And murmur in my heart my concerns to you

When I miss you
During a mid-summer night
I wish the rose fragrance
Wafts to your bedside
And the silk fan
Shoos away your tiredness

When I miss you
At a golden autumn dusk
I wish the roaming clouds at the edge of the sky
Bring me over to you

Missing you
Is a secret in my heart
Like rain
Each drop is a heart beat
Missing you
Is the honey in my heart
Like melodies
Each rings out my passion

Missing you
Is my most tender waiting for you

56. The Rebirth of a Tree

Spring breeze, on receiving the message from the leaves
Keeps silent
In silence, the tree extemporizes her dream-weaving

The breeze is tempted to tug at the tree's hands
But the tree hesitates for quite a while
The breeze says, what a fair pair
Of fine hands
The tree feels mesmerized

The breeze cuddles the tree
The tree begins to shiver
The breeze caresses the tree's twigs, whispering about the autumn
The tree sobs, tears dripping down onto her bosom

57. The Autumn Bride

We can't pin down the melting point between fire and water
But between draught and flood we can locate our homes
Let me bury the withered flower petals
And transplant into my heart the flowers in bloom or not yet

Hand in hand, we walk out into the deep autumn
Along the ancient-old path we fill the gap with falling sand
We weave the falling leaves into dowry and colored silk fabrics
And pin onto my alluring hair two maple leaves

After giving away gold bars and the land
We embrace each other at the lowest point of time
Guarding no more the peace of the virgin lake
Looking no more for the intricate reflections

Autumn wind trumpets for our wedding ceremony
Falling leaves dance in wind
Little birds sing in the deep valley
White clouds spread out wedding marshmallows

Extreme revelries feel mediocre
The clash of soul and flesh transcends into rapture
Autumn—autumn—autumnal bride
Gently lies wrapped in your arms

58. An Amorous Spring Night

Sexual love
Is a vital force God has gifted us
And forms the most beautiful scene

Gentle breeze
Roaring rain
A mermaid flipping the fin in the sea
Finally deep slumber in the moonlight

Then a new sky
And new bird-twittering
Sunlight appears more radiant
And the earth is strewn with massive blooms

59. Exorbitant Expectation

I long to, from your life
Pluck a rose that belongs to me

For this
I've cooked a tableful of
Valentine's day dinner

And then wait
—Silently wait
For you to present me the rose

The candle has burned out
Music ended, and the attenders parted
But I've never seen the rose

I want to say
I'm a real fool
Simply an idiot

I want to say
Your rose
I don't care about
But while saying this, tears stream down my face
They bloom out of my exorbitant expectation

60. There Is Such Love

There is such love
Which, when folded
Looks clean and neat
But never needs to be unfolded

There is such love
Which is flawed
Yet flavorful as rice wine
With endless fascination

There is such love
Which is far from you
But feels right by you
Vibrant with silent concerns
And hearty wishes

There is such love
With which your inspiration gushes like spring
Your talent is fulfilled
Your countenance glows
And Your life shines

There is such love
Which's too weighty for the feeling of longing
Too painful to utter it
Yet you never regret it for your whole life

61. Twin Flowers on One Stalk

What is called care
What is called longing
Daily concerning regards
Feel like clear spring water

What is an intimate
What is affection
Words out of empathy
Feel like sweet honey

What is called purity
What is called courage
White snowflakes
Are swirling in the air

What is passion
What is obsession
The clock of longing
Is ticking non-stop

A magpie
Perches on a tree branch
Waiting for
Love to happen in winter
Despite the rigid cold

Upon a snow-capped mountain
Blooms
A twin
Flower on one stalk

62. Understanding You

Why
Is your gaze
So wandering

Why
Is your eye expression
So roaming

Why
Is your soul
always drifting

So many years
Have elapsed
Why
Still
No one
Can understand you
But has left you
Alone
For so long and too long

Your gaze
Is obviously a call
Your eye expression
A search
Your soul
A quest
Your gaze
Hurts me
Your eye expression
Pains me
Your soul
Is a new-born baby
Pure like an angel

Let our gaze melt each other

Let our eye expressions warm each other
Let our souls embrace each other

I've brought spring along with me
To welcome you
I've brought the sun along with me
To embrace you
I've brought wings with me for you
So we can soar far and high

My dear
I am the one
Who understands you
Starting today
Let us accompany each other
To fly in this terrestrial world
Starting today
Let us hold hand in hand
Weave through the four seasons of life
No matter what harsh wind and rain
we will encounter
We cling firmly together

Starting today
Your gaze
Is my gaze
Your eye expression
My eye expression
Your soul
My soul
Because I'm the one who understands you
                        understands you

63. My Love

You follow me into the idyllic world
And weave through canola fields
Where flowers upon flowers
Are adorned by sunlight
While white clouds are poeticized in the azure sky
We tread on check after check of field soils

When I bend down
You can't see me
I wave my purple-colored silk kerchief
But are you able to get me
My love
Is as tender as the canola flowers
And as romantic as the silk kerchief

Let us board the sail
Drift in the sea
And skirt round the torrents and reefs
Let us berth at where fishes are fat and water is limpid
Far away from the terrestrial clamor

Only you understand me
And I understand you
Let us stay on the ISLAND
Use a conch to make rice
Use coral as ornaments
Then
We don't need to go to the other bank
We stay here together
To listen to the sea narrating its story
For hundreds and thousands of years.

64. Dancing

I step back, and you step forward
I step forward, and you step back
Swirling on the dance floor of love
To achieve the rhythmic beauty
As a price, we both are very careful

65. Promise

You are
The sky I look into
You are
Sky-high and cloud-plain
While my heart
Is as peaceful as a lake

My longing
Is like a could
And soundless
But always accompanies you

You are
The sea I gaze to
You are
Windless and tranquil
While my heart
Is as calm as the sea

My longing
Is like wind
And colorless
But always follows you

As my sky
You
Must be sky-high and clouds-plain
As my sea
You
Must be windless and tranquil

You
Are the scenery I admire
You
Are the concern lingering in my heart

Whether you are far or close

Please
Keep yourself visible or known
To me

This is
My only request
For you

Which can also
Be taken
As our promise

66. An Unusual Love

There is such love
That exists between two different genders

Its temperature is like that in spring
Depth, the big sea
Color, the blue sky
Taste, famous tea

Such love
Has nothing to do with
Age, marriage, social position, wealth, or worldly affairs

Its feeling toward each other is like a brook
That murmurs along
Its understanding of each other is like spring drizzle
That nurtures flora quietly
Its love of each other is like willow strings
That caress you in the wind
Its yearning between each other is like air
That permeates everywhere

But
He cooks his own rice
She fries her own vegs
The daily affairs
Is of each own

They are attached
Like reflections in a lake
They are detached
A love knot tied to the azure sky
A couple of angels
Winging at the edge of clouds

67. Let Us Hold Our Hands Forever

New Year's chimes
Peal to hail the break of a new dawn
From one heart to the other
Wafts balmy wind

We have gone through winter
And ventured spring
Oath is untrustworthy
Promises are hardly kept
But only silence is the safe island for love

Summer is scorching
Autumn is not here yet
Let us
Hold our hands
And take the future road
Together

Hand in hand
Even if we run
From tsunami, against volcanoes, or out of ruins
We form the most beautiful scene

Let us
Hold our hands
A day of our hands holding will last a year
A year of our hands holding, a lifetime

Let us hold our hands
To turn brambles into an oasis
Let us hold our hands
To turn our dreams into reality
Let us hold our hands
To head into the consummate autumn

68. Come on Over

I'm here
Not to inflame my passion
But to let you feel my warmth

I'm here
Not to get myself deeply involved
But to make you feel at ease

I'm here
Not to date you
But to meet you

I'm here
With my hair cascading in azure blue
I'm here with an ardent heart
The white color
Is my dress

If you understand me
If you are a match
for this blue and white
Come on over then

As long as you come over
I will surely come over too

69. Why

Why do birds sing
But I speak less and less
I do have something to say
But feel reluctant to utter it

Why do rills romp along
But I keep backing up
I do want to reach the other bank
But dare not cross the river

Exhausted
I fumble through the loneliness of the night
Wanting to force some smiles
But instead tears rolling down
The best poems
Have halted
For Muse goddess
No longer visits me

Where on earth
Is the mistake
Thrills and joys
No longer adore me

Time and again, I ask myself
But the answerless question
Forms my last song

70. Autumn Roses

Treading the autumn leaves
You walk to me with a charming smile
You kindle the autumn
To set the world aflame
And ripple the still water

You wave your hand
To turn the decadent into fairy tales
And quietly set sail the legends
The autumn splendor is not a dream

The leaves are no longer green
Yet fully beaten by weather and vicissitudes
In the autumn chill, only you blossom
The warmth of spring
Two little deer are bounding in the street

No need to envy the height birds can fly to
No need to dream of being a millionaire
I only want to quaff
In such a late fall
Rich and mellow wine with you

Maple leaves bear witness that each story
Montages the glistening of purest teardrops
Both of you are leading characters
With a rose tree in the distance ahead
Blooming toward the sun against the wind

71. Deep Autumn Provoked Deep Longing

Even air seems heavy
Roses bloom silently
And the feeling of longing permeates quietly

In the air, the geese flutter their wings toward the south
My longing turns into propitious clouds to fly to you

Time span
Cannot be measured by days
The increasing sense of longing
Stretches each second to a thousand years
—Daytime is longing and nighttime longing too

This deep autumn
My longing is like evening twilight
Painfully burning the clouds
And dying red the edge of the sky

72. Love Found through the Internet

I can stop my pen
But I can hardly stop longing for you
I can quit the internet
But I can hardly quit the dolorous urge to see you

Seeing each other on-screen
Is a daily scene
You are right there in front of me
But I can hardly touch you to feel your cool

You walk here and there before me
Each movement triggers my melancholy
The Yin and Yang of my heart mood
Is measured by your footsteps

How I want to be that mouse in your hand
So, I can know the orientation of your heart

73. To Give Up

Using my pain
I make a colorful kite
While flying it, I let off the towing line
And give up the idea of pulling it back

Let love turn into flaming roses
And spread them into a waterfall
The cascade buries the petals
Forever

Looking up into the sky
Clouds in motion on all sides
But I lock up the motion in my dream

The roadside plants
Bear undeserved flourishing names
Before the sun rises
They wipe out their tears

Although my love
Is unpredictable for tomorrow
Once happened
I'll never bewail a regret

The blue poem
Is elusive
Then why not lull it into sleep
Like last night

VI. A Hand Fan

74. A Hand Fan

One side is spring, the other autumn
You are that spring, me that autumn

Spring and autumn
A separation only a paper-thickness apart
Yet feels as if in different world corners

Spring and autumn
Often not much difference in temperature
Yet never belong
To the same season

75. Famous Wine

 If you place it in a wine cabinet
And look at it
You 'll feel a sense of possession

If you open it
Its aroma will fade away
If you drink it
The sense of possession will be lost

76. The Thermos Bottle

How I wish
To strip off
Your outer metal cover
So
The hot flow in you can surge

How I wish
To pry open
Your firm cork
So
The ardent passion in you can billow

Don't
Insulate your heart in the shell
Let me
Nestle in your embrace

Dare
You
Hide
From me

I will
Crumble your vacuum flask
And let it bloom
On my palm

77. The Drinking Water Bottle

What 's poured in, hot water
What's poured out, cold water

You suppress
Your own ardor
To satiate
Everyone's thirst

You are inflicted with hotness
And coldness
But no one feels
What you feel

78. Startled

Startled
Oh, it's a bird
That has fluttered away from a tree

I wonder
If I've startled it
Or it has startled me

What a bold bird
I've turned back to look at it
But it flies straight away

79. Bridge

Without you
People long for one
With you
People forget your significance
Many people have trodden on you
Yet you've never complained about it
You help people cross the river
Yet you take this as your responsibility

80. The Fall Wind

I meant to weave the fall leaves
Into a net
To catch
The falling fall

Yet to the contrary
The fall falls harder

81. Your Leaves and My Water

Your leaves
Have fallen into my yard
My water
Has wetted your lawn

Even standing in between
I still can't tell
Which side is me
And which side is you

If you want
I can pick up the leaves
And return them to you
But you will not be able to
Return the water to me

82. Mood

In the front yard
Tulips are blooming

In the back yard
Weeds are overgrown

The front yard
And the back yard
Which reflects my mood

A few birdies
Are hop-dancing to their own singing

83. A Woman Who Does not Use a Cell Phone

Birds
Are most beautiful when taking off
Flowers
Most fragrant when in bloom
Time spent without a cell phone
Most anxious

Contemporary life
Is very exhausting
How I wish
I could enter
That legendary
        American village

Where people
Go out working at sunrise
And return home at sunset
Rejecting modern electronic devices

Where there are no drugs, guns, nuclear weapons, or wars
No corrupt officials or prostitutes
And no cellphone ringing

Where
Babies give the most beautiful smiles in sleep
And fathers who do not use cell phones
Are the best fathers

Sunlight
        Sea waves
                Beaches
                        Wood huts in the forests
                                What a paradise

Outside of the village
A woman who does not use a cell phone
Stands on the horizon

And gazes into the distance
She for the flying birds
    And blooming flowers
      Keeps nodding

84. Leaves and Birds

A wingless leaf
Can fly high
Because of the wind it resorts to

A landed bird
Can take off again
Because of the two wings it possesses

Leaves are born earthbound
Yet, birds, celestial

85. The Very Same

There is this tree
That has grown very, very tall
A leaf
Perches upon
Its very, very tall tip

The leaf dwells against the boundless sky
And dwarfs all in its downward view
It accompanies the clouds
Plays peekaboo with the moon sister
And chases the sun brother

Autumn wind blows over
No matter how she prays
The greenness can no longer sustain
Which gradually turns yellow
And then red

And then finally
Drifts down into the stream
And flow to the distance

The shape of that leaf
The color of that leaf
And the experience of that leaf
Are the very same
As my heart

86. Railway Tracks

You are one of the two tracks
I am the other
We are parallel
And have never intersected each other
When a train comes along
We sustain its weight together
When a storm strikes
We stay firm together

Railway Tracks
You are one of the two
I am the other
We are parallel
We don't have to intersect each other

When train is gone
We nod to each other
When a storm is over
We give each other an understanding smile

87. Lotus Root Is the Mercy Buddha

Under the sky
And above the earth
You are a celestial fairy
Who has turned into a lotus seed
And descended into a lonely pond

The lotus seed
Is self-awakening and self-purifying
A loner in the loneliness

Silt
Cannot hinder it
From growing into a lotus root
Turbid water
Cannot stop it
From blooming

With eyes closed
It sits amid the green leaves meditating
And on the sepals reciting Buddhist sutra
The lotus' obsession remains attached
Whereas its pocketed roots broken

Dauntless of sunlight
It glows charming—
Charming, but not gaudy
It wafts fragrance—
And is proud, but not arrogant
It makes all other flowers shy

It comes out of silt unsoiled
Clean as ice and pure as jade
Transcends mundane people

Whether white
Or pink
All lotuses are the Mercy Buddha

88. This Is not Roving

I will leave like this
And never return
For the biography of a hero
Never carries tears or crying

I will leave like this
And never return
No matter how loud the noise behind is
Or what weird croaks the river frogs make

I will walk on like this—
Treading on the fallen leaves
I will walk into the distance
And with the usual persistence
To let go the past sorrows
I will walk into the setting-sun lights

I will walk on like this—
I will walk into the village of others'
And take it as my own hometown
I will walk into the forest
To rebuild my home
This is not roving

VII. The Scarf of the Moonlight

89. The Scarf of the Moonlight

Lying on the softness
I close my eyes to gaze at the stars
But see you standing in snow and ice

I use the moonlight
To weave a scarf
And let the chilly wind to bring it to you

—No
I will let the wind to bring me over
So I could in person
Wrap the warm scarf
Around your neck

And so I can see how your face
Turn into
A happy smiling sun

90. Gui Fei, the Imperial Beauty, Is Drunk

Open a 100-year-old vintage
And its aroma will spread over a 10-mile-long grassland

Raising the cup to the world's remotest corner
I say, bottom up, bottom up
For the two lotus flowers blooming side by side

In chasing the colorful cloud, the wind murmurs
In half-awoken and half-drunken state
Excellent wine, excellent wine
The Imperial beauty is drunk
And will let the intoxication hang over for eons

91. Glamorous Photos

Paint your face lead-white
And add two fake eyelashes on it
And put on the costume used by large customers
And style your hair

The heavy cosmetic young look
The rushed-out beauty
The photographer's instructions
And your dramatical poses in the flashlights
Plus a forced smile

The magic digital camera
Can quickly
Create hundreds of wondrous belles
That are more glamorous than film stars in dream stills
And that too well intoxicate yourself

92. The Firefly

Flashing and flickering
To the dark night
It brings sparks of light
That is a firefly

It is
Not as bright as the street lamp
Nor the moon in the sky
But it flashes
Earnestly

It is a star children chase
It glows in the dark
It vivifies the night with a hovering fairy

The petite firefly
Has flown into
People's time-preserved memories

93. Fish Begin to Chuckle

The blue orb
Is the globe
The blue water
The sea

This earth
Is 71 percent water-covered
29 percent, land

Humans
Live on land
Fish
In water

When humans say
We are the master of this globe
Fish begin to chuckle

94. Heavy Snow

When the sun is on vacation
Soft snow
Will occupy some places on the earth

When the sun is back
Tears rain down for a month
The tears
Have washed the streets
And watered the lawns
And spruced up the earth for the smile of spring

95. Size

In my birth country
I wear large-sized clothes
After I come to America
Even the medium-sized
Seems a bit too loose

So reluctantly
I turn to small size
Which proves
The small size
Is the right size for me

96. Teeth

Poor physical health
Results in poor dental health

Gum surgery
Costs thousands
And a tooth implant
Costs extra thousands

Finally
You have got
A golden mouth and oracular utterances

97. Dust

The earth
Is a speck of dust in the galaxy

The galaxy
A speck of dust in the universe

Living on a speck of dust
One can never be big

Fame and fortune
Money and power
Are specks of dust in other specks of dust

A speck of dust
Will eventually settle

98. Flowers in Tranquility

All flowers
Are beautiful

Some flowers
Are fond of enticing bees and seducing butterflies
Others
Are never so

There is one species
That wafts fragrance in tranquility
She
Only belongs to
The green leaves that support her

Because
She and the green leaves
Have grown together
And experienced together the natural inflections

She knows what gratefulness is
And what loyalty is

This flower in the tranquility
Is like the flower in the realm of Zen
The flower in the realm of Zen
Is the flower of a woman

99. The Blooming and Falling of a Flower

The blooming of every flower
Is what a dream expects
The blooming of every flower
Is what a life ventures

When a flower blooms
It's unpredictable if it will fruit
But when a flower blooms
It's certain that it will eventually fall

People say women are like flowers
And young girls are the most tender flowers

But in this world no flower does not wither
And no young girl does not age
The natural blooming and calm falling
Are the romance of life

A pretty woman with grey hair
Is gazing at the withered flowers on a tree
When a gust of wind
Sweeps off the flower petals

That woman
Smiles in the wind
Her smile is as charming
As a blooming daisy

100. The Light of Poetry

Amazing! Poetry is a luminous thing
That only needs someone to light up

You come
With a smile
And a rose
Your smile has kindled the light
And your rose has kindled the poetic inspiration

Thus poetry is born in the light
And you are reborn in the poetry
And I am reborn in the poetry

And in the poetry, I write poetry
My poetry is the live painting of your life
My poetry is the reflection
That reflects your light

You are the light, the brightest light
I am the poetry, the most beautiful poetry

Therefore, you and I
In the realm of poetry
Bathe together in the poetic light

Bing Hua

Bing Hua is the pen name of Lihua Lu, who is also known as Rose Lu. She is an accountant in Maryland, vice president of the Chinese Poetry Association, content director of *Poetry Hall*. She has been called "the queen of love poetry" and "a rose in the poetic world", and her poetic style is called the "Bing Hua Style". Her poems are so influential that they are considered "Bing Hua Phenomenon".

She began writing poetry during the 1980s. Her publications include *February's Rose* (2022), *Selected Poems of Bing Hua*, a bilingual work in Chinese and English published in 2019/2020, *This is Love* (2013), and *Roses by the Stream* with a Chinese edition published in 2008 and a bilingual edition published in 2019. She co-edited Best Modern and Contemporary Chinese Poetry (2021), *Best Overseas Chinese Poetry* (2021), *Penetrating Time and Space—A Poetry Group of William Marr* (2022). Two of her poems, "A Hand Fan" and "Neither out of Flighty or Levity" won the "Belief in Love" Golden Award in the 31st World Congress Poets Contest. "The Lotus Obsession" won the Butterfly Golden Award in the 1st World Chinese Language Love Poems Contest. She was judged an excellent poet by the Poetry Network in 2016. Bing Hua won the China New Regression Poets award in 2017, and was a Pushcart Prize nominee in 2015 and 2021.

Yingcai Xu

Yingcai Xu is a teacher, translator, and poet. The courses he has taught include classical and modern Chinese languages, classical and modern Chinese literature, Chinese cinema, Chinese calligraphy theory and practice, and Translation. He once went to teach at McMaster University, Canada, while taking Canadian literature courses there. Later, he came to DePaul University to study English and American literature, where he established the university's Chinese program. He has about a dozen translation books published. Some of them have turned to be government gifts and some university teaching materials. In translation, he has a three-word principle, *accuracy, individuality, and cohesion.* While trying to achieve an accurate rendering of the original text, he pursues the original spirit and a translation highly acceptable by mother-tongue readers. Besides, he has edited and co-edited nearly a dozen translation books. Yingcai Xu is also a poet. His poetry publications include *Poetic South, Inspiration from Nature—Poems by Yingcai Xu in Chinese and English,* and *We Are Here Painting.* He is now preparing to have a collection of haikus published. Yingcai Xu is also the President of the Chinese Poetry Association and an editor-in-chief of Poetry Hall, a Chinese-and-English bilingual journal. His poetic philosophy is: use simple, appealing, and imagination-evoking language to create vivid and poetic-sense-infused poems that come directly from the heart and the physical world and create a lasting and glittering effect of *yijing* or artistic conception.

www.ingramcontent.com/pod-product-compliance
Lightning Source LLC
Chambersburg PA
CBHW021147090426
42740CB00008B/987